How to bring up intelligent teens:

A parenting manual on how to raise smart teenagers

Leon Fleischer

Table of contents

Introduction

Parenting comes with a job description that includes worry. And if your child has scholastic difficulties, such as reading, writing, or math, you've probably worried a bit about the future.

Of course, you wouldn't say it out, but have you ever questioned in your mind:

Is my child simply... stupid?
Will she spend the rest of her days in the basement?
Should he join the circus? Ah, but. Just now, the circus called it a day. What is he going to do?

If you've ever had such or similar ideas, don't feel embarrassed.

When students with average to above average intelligence found it difficult to keep up with their peers, it was simple to label them as lazy, unmotivated, or all of the above. It must be the students' fault, not the school's if they couldn't keep up with the rest of the class.

The experts in the field of learning differences, also known as "disabilities," knew better. Yet these pupils frequently slipped through the cracks of the educational system.

Children with unidentified learning differences may have struggled to learn throughout their entire lives if they weren't given the support they required. They probably believed they were ignorant, inept, and dumb without evidence to the contrary. What else could account for the fact that they labored twice as hard and completed projects three times more slowly than everyone else?

Rewind to the present day. There are several reasons why your teen could need special education services, one of which is a specific learning disability (SLD). This could be a problem with visual or auditory processing, dyslexia, dysgraphia, or another condition.

The most important thing to remember is that the following are NOT included in the Individuals with Disabilities Act's (IDEA) definition of a particular learning disability:

- Learning issues that are predominantly brought on by an intellectual handicap are not included in specific learning disabilities.

- No SLD is linked to a lack of effort, intellect, or drive.

Therefore, if your teen has an IQ below 80, you may need to start planning for future adjustments.

Indeed, academic achievements are probably not indicative of smarty pants status. Still not. But learning doesn't have to be a struggle that lasts a lifetime with the correct programs and support. Because he is not, your teen doesn't need to feel foolish, ignorant, or inept. She's not. Possibly even talented.

That secret knowledge? It only has to be tapped.

And the best facilitator is you, dear parent. I focused more on HOW to improve your child's aptitude to learn throughout this book.

Chapter 1

PROBLEMS YOUR CHILD MAY BE HAVING IN SCHOOL

Anyone who has experienced adolescence may remember the highs and lows of attending school. There are several frequent situations that you may want to think about while your teen is going through a difficult or stressful time:

1. Brand-new starts

Beginning at a new school is thrilling, but for some, it may be a bit challenging because of the strange surroundings and lots of new people. A fantastic technique to help your adolescent get ready is to talk positively about the experience and mention all the awesome new friends and activities they'll have.

2. Having to make important choices

Your teen will have to make a lot of important decisions during their final years of high school, and they might feel under pressure to already be on the right career path. Tell your teen that there is information available to help them understand their options, whether they are interested in science, design, or even taking a gap year, and assure them that you will support them as they make any difficult choices.

3. Harassment

Bullying is a terrible experience for a teen, whether it involves being called names, feeling excluded, or being contacted online. It can be challenging for parents to deal with because it's not always obvious that their teen is going through this. Find out what to look out for and how you can help if you've noticed that they're acting differently and are concerned that they might be being bullied.

4. Peer pressure and friendships

Friends turn into your teenager's primary support system during high school. They help them develop a sense of identity, try new things, and feel a sense of belonging outside the family unit. However, when young people spend all day every day with each other, there's bound to be an occasional clash. If you develop your teenagers' self-esteem and confidence they are more likely to improve their ability to stand up for themselves and others, building positive friendships throughout high school.

5. Trouble focusing

Whilst social media can help your teen connect and unwind, the constant notifications and the 'always on nature of it can sometimes get a bit distracting. You can help them focus by suggesting social media-free times and by keeping TV and music volumes down while they're studying.

6. Exam Anxiety

Your teenager might experience pressure leading up to the Year 12 exams from a variety of sources. The best person to assess how your adolescent is feeling is your adolescent, but as a parent, you can be there to support and validate them while keeping an eye out for warning signs they might not be aware of.

SIGNS THAT YOUR TEENS MAY BE GOING THROUGH A DIFFICULT TIME

If you're not sure how your adolescent is adjusting, keep an eye out for these changes in their attitude or behavior:

- Being distant or disengaged,
- Losing interest in activities they typically enjoy,
- Changing their eating or sleeping patterns, and
- Feeling grumpy or agitated.

Additional ways to help your teen
Building your teen's confidence and assisting them in developing a strong sense of self can be a great way to help them succeed in school.

Teenagers can really benefit from adults showing an active interest in how they are doing and from open, honest conversations.

Talk to your teen about the situation if they seem more stressed than usual. Give them some helpful coping techniques or point them in the direction of an app that can help people manage their anxiety.

Talk to your doctor if you're still concerned, and look into some other options.

Additionally, you may make connections with other parents who share your circumstances. Any problem or situation that you and your adolescent are having may be discussed.

Chapter 2

WHAT MAKES ADOLESCENTS INTELLIGENT?

It's a challenging question because some children are street smart while others are book smart. Some people construct massive block buildings, while others use poetry and prose to create word paintings. Some people are elected president of the school, while others know exactly how to cheer you up.

The general capacity to process information that supports learning, understanding, reasoning, and problem-solving is reflected in intelligence.
It influences a wide range of common behaviors.
I'll concentrate on why teenage children differ in intelligence and how to bring out the best in them because every child is different.

1. Environment or Heredity?

Despite the fact that more than 80% of the variance in adult intelligence is determined by heredity, each succeeding generation scores higher on IQ tests, emphasizing the significance of environmental factors. Why the apparent inconsistency?

The underlying presumption in this paradox is that environment and genes are unrelated, which is absurd to say out loud. The majority of the work that the environment performs is attributed to genes.
It's a positive or negative cycle if IQ affects the environment and the environment affects IQ.

The effects of the environment on intelligence deteriorate over time. For instance, an infant's IQ reaches its peak between six and twelve months after entering a preschool enrichment program. The child's IQ starts to decline after they leave that environment.

An adolescent will act differently if you take him out of a positive atmosphere and place him in a negative one. He may pick wiser pals or watch more instructive television. But since there are fewer possibilities than in the ideal setting, his IQ will gradually decline over time.

2. Intelligence Assessment

How much weight should we give to those mysterious IQ scores?

I don't believe there's much value in attempting to gauge a child's IQ unless they seem unusually smart, precocious, or not growing normally. Individual test results are often taken too seriously by people.

Whether a youngster is inquisitive, likes to play and learn via role-playing, and its content is a stronger indicator than intelligence level.

The only factor, however, that accurately predicts how economically and socially successful 14-year-olds will be as adults is their IQ score.

3. Brain Food

The majority of the brain's development is finished by adolescence, yet it still makes important connections. Adolescence is the most crucial period for eating healthily, second only to infancy. Another time when a balanced diet is crucial for brain development is now.

Teenagers need a broad range of meals from the five dietary groups—vegetables, fruit, grains, dairy, and protein—that are considered to be healthy.

Nutrients included in healthy diets are crucial for growth and development throughout puberty.
Teenagers should restrict their intake of high-sodium, high-fat, and high-sugar meals as well as low-fiber foods and beverages.

4. Develop mental strength

Every night, read something together to develop young brains. Encourage your adolescent to learn an instrument by fostering his or her hobbies and curiosities.

The "Mozart effect," which claims that classical music listening raises certain IQ scores, is most likely exaggerated.
Children who are raised in families where talking, listening, and reading are commonplace likely to have higher IQs and do more academically.

More time spent with your adolescent may result in stronger parent-child bonds and better mental development.

Teenagers who are left alone to watch TV or play video games will not do as well. Encourage conversation and active learning.

Teenagers need space and freedom to play and explore as they mature. Don't push your own hobbies on them; instead, engage them in activities that require discipline and concentrated attention such as sports or music. Even if Dad loved hockey as a teen, it doesn't mean his own teens would.

The learning methods and interests of every teen are different. We must not overlook desire, bravery, and diligence while becoming intelligent, since they are equally crucial for success. Don't forget to impart learning skills to them.
Few individuals even recognize their potential, much less use it. Encourage

teenagers to acquire the mindset and skills necessary to use their brains to the fullest.

Teenagers' performance may be enhanced if we consider how they think. We get significantly better outcomes when we tailor our instruction to the capacities of the students.

Utilize it or lose it

The development of intellect should be a lifetime endeavor since the early environmental impacts fade. Your adolescent should be off to a flying start if they are fed a balanced diet and encouraged to make the most use of their special talents.

If you can even briefly increase a teen's capacity for learning, the lessons they absorb might stick with them for 20 or 30 years. You may use certain abilities throughout your whole life. Even if they can't improve their teen's IQ permanently,

parents may have a long-term impact on
how well he does at work and how much
money he makes.

Chapter 3

WAYS TO INSPIRE THEM TO STUDY

Do you find it difficult to inspire your teenager?
It's normal for parents to worry.
After all, raising teenagers is not simple.
While you don't want to be a dictator, you still want your teenagers to grow up to be successful, responsible adults.

If you stop policing and lecturing your teenagers, what will happen?
Will they ever form the wholesome, lifelong habits required for success?

What you should bear in mind is as follows:
Your teen's ability to develop intrinsic motivation won't be aided by your micromanaging and nagging.

Your teenagers may be able to pass an exam with its assistance, but what will happen when they are in college and you are not there to mentor them?

The key to inspiring adolescent motivation is to support and encourage the growth of self-discipline.
Your teenagers will therefore achieve academic success and, more crucially, develop the self-assurance and mentality necessary for success in all facets of life.

Teenagers may be motivated. Using the following techniques, you may assist your teenagers in acquiring intrinsic drive right now.

13 methods for inspiring your adolescent

In order to help your teens without micromanaging them, let's look at some suggestions for motivating teenagers.

1. Pay more attention to the process than the result.

Although doing well in school and extracurricular activities are important, there is more to life than that.

The qualities your teen develops along the way, such as responsibility, perseverance, resilience, and hard work, are what matter most.
Encourage your adolescent to concentrate on improving his or her study habits and motivation.

If your teenagers don't accomplish their objectives, assist them in finding areas where they may succeed while focusing on the work they put out.
You may remark, for instance, "I hope you're proud of yourself for practicing every day even if you didn't make the football team. You demonstrated tenacity and grit.

How do you believe you can practice more successfully the next time?

Your teens will be less inclined to avoid problems and more eager to attempt new things if you place more emphasis on the process.

Here are some other suggestions for motivating your adolescent to adopt a process-oriented approach to learning:

- Talk about the advantages of learning and studying that go beyond achieving high marks.

- Explain how time, effort, and dedication are necessary for fulfilling occupations and pastimes.

- Praise your teen for their efforts rather than just for exceptional performance.

- Talk about your teen's goals and aspirations and demonstrate how you're pursuing your own dreams (even if it means that you might fail along the way).

Every parent wants their adolescent to do well in school.

Parents and teenagers don't often prefer procedures over results, thus this is not a natural propensity. However, if you change your perspective and assist your teenagers in doing the same, you'll enable them to get the desire and self-control they need to succeed in life.

Then, positive results are certain to follow!

2. Respect your adolescent's independence

Your adolescents are coming to terms with who they are as individuals and learning how to navigate the world.

Your adolescents may not yet be adults, but growing up naturally includes the desire for more freedom and autonomy.

What is the issue?
The majority of teens are subject to rigid guidelines and timetables. Their everyday schedules are often out of their control.
Many teens experience frustration, helplessness, and eventually a lack of motivation as a consequence.

Now, I'm not advocating allowing your teens to act in any way they choose. However, it's crucial to provide teens with some autonomy so they'll be more inclined to put in extra effort and finish what they start.

Setting rules and consequences jointly is a simple approach to respecting your adolescent's autonomy.
They'll see that you value their viewpoints. Then, they'll have more incentive to respect

your limits and those that both of you have established.

Avoid the temptation to tell a teen, "I know what's best for you," while trying to inspire them.
Perhaps you really do know what is best for your teens. However, they will grow into responsible adults when you assist them in accepting more autonomy.

3.   Encourage   compassionate communication

Even if their opinions differ from your own, speak with your teenagers and pay attention to what they have to say.
Encourage free discussion and swap boring lectures with compassionate, reassuring exchanges.

When your teen approaches you with an issue, resist the impulse to jump in and provide unsolicited counsel. You may still provide direction and counseling, but you should say less and listen more.

In other words, engage in active listening while paying close attention to your adolescent.

Your teenagers will experience understanding rather than criticism or judgment when you foster this sort of pleasant atmosphere. Then, they'll be more inclined to open up to you about their true life.

You probably won't be surprised to learn that research indicates that teens with tight family ties and open communication are less likely to have behavioral issues.

You could be thinking, "I'd want to speak to my adolescents more, but they never want to talk to me," at this point.

Having frequent mealtime conversations with teens is a fantastic method to encourage honest, compassionate communication. Make family meals a priority since 80% of teens believe they are more likely to chat with their parents during mealtimes.

4. Encourage your teen's pursuits

Do your teenagers like activities like dance, music, or sports outside of the classroom?
In that case, excellent!
While other activities and interests are important for your teen's general growth, academics are crucial.

Your teenagers gain self-motivation and acquire other life skills when they devote time to a hobby.
Don't dismiss your teenagers' interests as a waste of time. Your teenagers could grow enraged and bitter if you do it.

Therefore, encourage your teenagers to explore their hobbies while promoting a balanced lifestyle. You won't have to worry about how to inspire a teenager if you follow this advice.

Do you have any doubts regarding your adolescents' interests?
Start by paying attention to and watching them. What can seem to be time squandered on social media may really be a love for media creation or video editing.

5. Be an excellent role model for your teenager.

Adults procrastinate too, whether it's by letting the laundry build up, postponing that long overdue dental visit, or continually pressing the snooze button.

Being a parent is challenging, and nobody expects you to be flawless.
Still, whether consciously or unconsciously, your adolescents are observing you and modeling their behavior after you.

Your teenagers can have a difficult time acting differently if you find it difficult to be motivated for the things that count.

However, your adolescents will be more likely to adopt these traits if they see you being diligent, accountable, and disciplined.

Here are just a few ideas about how to be a good role model for your teens:
Create a culture in your home where making errors is acceptable. Share your aspirations and failures, and don't be afraid to take on new challenges.

Avoid delaying as much as you can. Do it straight away if there's a quick chore you can do in a few minutes.

Take care of your physical and emotional health to show that you have a comprehensive approach to motivation.

6. Talk to and about your adolescent in a favorable manner.

Why aren't you able to concentrate better like your brother?

"I've heard that Ben, your classmate, received all As. You can do it too if he can, I'm sure.

Comparing your adolescent to their siblings or classmates is alluring. However, this may lead to poor self-esteem and even animosity in your adolescent rather than inspiring them.

As frequently as you can, use encouraging language with your teenagers. Celebrate each individual's skills and help them understand that working hard can be enjoyable and rewarding.

Here's one more piece of advice.

Your teenagers will also perceive any comparisons you make when you say things such as, "When I was your age... " They'll

think you don't attach to or comprehend their circumstances or viewpoint.
So, do your best to refrain from saying anything of this kind as much as you can.

7. Encourage good practices

Never undervalue the importance of getting a good night's sleep if you want to know how to encourage a teenager.
Anyone who is fatigued finds it difficult to be motivated.

Help your teen establish a schedule that allows for ample time for rest since research indicates that teens require 8 to 10 hours of sleep every day to perform at their best.

Exercise and nutrition are important, too. Teenagers who practice healthy behaviors have better stress management and self-control.

When encouraging your adolescent to adopt healthy behaviors, pay particular attention to the following:

- Create a daily schedule

- Regular exercise

- Turn off all electronics before bed.

- Limiting your caffeine intake

- Consume a healthy diet.

Keep in mind that if you practice self-care, your adolescent will be more inclined to do so as well.

8. Steer clear of imposing both incentives and penalties.

It appears easy to inspire youngsters by using prizes and penalties.

In fact, parents often ask me questions like, "Won't my adolescents study harder if they receive additional time playing video games for excellent marks and lose their phone privileges for low grades?"

But here's something you should know...
According to research, incentives and penalties don't increase motivation in the long run. They may force your teenagers to study more for an impending test, but they won't instill in them the virtue of perseverance and hard effort.
In addition, outcomes are prioritized above processes in terms of incentives and penalties.

We want to foster in our teenagers a love of learning and taking on difficulties, as we discussed previously.
Therefore, if you're wondering how to encourage a teenager, steer clear of using incentives and punishments in favor of the advice in this book.

9. Allow natural consequences to play out.

Teenagers shouldn't be micromanaged by their parents. They should not, however, get away with anything.
Your adolescents must learn from their mistakes because they have repercussions.

Every parent wants to keep their children safe, but when practical, they should let events play out naturally.
For instance, don't do it for your teenagers if they don't put their filthy clothes in the hamper. They will be compelled to put on their soiled clothing again once they are out of clean ones.

And if your adolescent fails the test? Avoid the impulse to request a retake of the test from the instructor. For success the second time around, your adolescents must develop better study habits.

I am aware that you wish to save your teenagers from needless suffering and heartbreak.

However, you may prevent annoying power battles if you let them experience natural consequences rather than telling them, "I told you so."

Additionally, they will learn the value of having a strong sense of self and making informed decisions.

10. Look for a mentor

Did you know that students who have mentors have higher success rates?

It's great that your teenagers (hopefully) love and respect you. Still, it's beneficial that they get a fresh perspective from someone outside the family.

It's especially helpful for your teens to have a mentor when there's a conflict between you and them.

A mentor will be able to empower your teens to understand the situation from different points of view so that it will be easier to arrive at a solution.

A mentor could be a coach, teacher, neighbor, or even a family friend. It might also be a professional success and life coach for teens, which is a large part of the job i perform.

11. Equip your teen with valuable organizational tools

Your adolescent desires success. It's simply that having to balance increasing social and academic obligations might be challenging.
As a result, your adolescent uses movies, games, and social media as an escape rather than working through his or her lengthy to-do list.

You're left wondering how to encourage a teen in this circumstance.

Some essential organizational advice can be helpful if your teen is feeling defeated and frustrated. Start with these two basic abilities:

A. Slackening

By dividing challenging school assignments into smaller action items, this technique makes them feel more manageable.
If your teenagers have a big project to finish, assist them in "chunking" the work into manageable, one-at-a-time tasks.

B. Making lists

Encourage your teenagers to jot down any pertinent details, such as homework assignments, due dates, items to bring, and test dates.
By doing this, students will remember crucial dates and feel more in charge of the tasks at hand.

Your teens need to develop organizational and planning abilities just as adults do in order to be responsible.
They'll be more self-motivated if you provide them with the appropriate tools and techniques.

12. Prevent motivational speeches

Reading student motivational quotes might sometimes provide your teenagers with the instant inspiration boost they need to finish a task.

Pep speeches seldom succeed in keeping your teenagers motivated over the long run, however.
Why?
Because, at least in the eyes of your teenagers, even the most well-intended pep sessions often end up turning into lectures. What you intend to be motivating advice may come off as nagging or even reprimanding.

Instead of giving your teens motivational speeches, use the advice in this book to encourage them to find their own sources of a drive.

13. Create frameworks and routines with your adolescent.

You can't alter your life unless you change a daily habit. The key to your success may be discovered in the actions you do each day.
J. C. Maxwell

Want to give your adolescents the incentive they need to succeed while avoiding pointless conflict?
Establish and adhere to family routines.
A constant framework gives teens the best chance for success while giving them the room they need to develop their sense of autonomy.

Establishing routines for your family with your adolescents is the key to making them enjoyable and successful. Create a weekly and daily schedule that works for everyone by working together.

Remember to schedule time for extracurricular activities, hobbies, enjoyable family time, and other vital obligations as well. Include key tasks like study time and housework.

Maybe your teen wants to volunteer one Saturday a month or make supper for the family every Sunday.
Include them as often as you can in family activities since they are a great method to inspire each other to succeed in all facets of life.